CMT 4 Prep
Grade 4 Cloze Reading
Third Edition

by Jonathan D. Kantrowitz

Edited by Ralph R. Kantrowitz

Item Code RAS 2273 • Copyright © 2009 Queue, Inc.

Queue, Inc., 80 Hathaway Drive, Stratford, CT 06615
(800) 232-2224 • Fax: (800) 775-2729 • www.qworkbooks.com

Table of Contents

FILL IN THE MISSING WORD

Filling in the missing words is what this book is all about.

You will read a sentence that has had a word taken out. There will be a blank like this _____ where the word was. Your job will be to pick which word belongs in the blank.

You will need to pick which word makes the most sense in each sentence with a blank. You will be given five choices. Fill in the missing word by circling the letter of the correct answer. Here's an example with just two answer choices:

1. The _____ comes up every day.   a) song   b) sun

Read the sentence and the answer choices. Does a "song" come up every day? That doesn't sound right. Does the "sun" come up every day? That does make sense. The correct choice is **b**, sun. Circle the correct answer like this: (b) sun

Here is another one with four choices:

2. I read a _____ to my little brother last night.

    a) cook   b) look
    c) book   d) back

Read each of the answer choices. Try reading each one in the sentence. Which answer makes the most sense? It is **c**, book. That's what you would read to someone.

OK, now try these on your own:

3. In the winter, she loves to go _____ on the frozen pond near her house.

    a) swimming   b) skiing   e) dancing
    c) biking   d) skating

What do you do on ice? The answer to 3 is **d**, skating.

4. The fireman _____ a ladder to rescue the cat.

    a) chased   b) climbed   e) lit
    c) painted   d) walked

What do you do with a ladder? The answer to 4 is **b**, climbed.

Now here is one that is a little harder:

5. It was the middle of summer. The sun was high in the sky. Nothing was moving. It was very _____.

    a) raining   b) cloudy   e) windy
    c) hot   d) cold

"The sun was high in the sky" tells you that it wasn't **a**, raining or **b**, cloudy. "It was the middle of summer" tells you that it probably wasn't **d**, cold. Choice **e**, windy, is a possible answer, but "nothing was moving" doesn't fit with "windy." The best choice is **c**, hot.

Sometimes the right answer depends on what follows the blank. For example, look at the following question and answer choices:

6. My favorite room in my house is the _____. Everyone gathers there while my mom cooks dinner. It's warm and cozy and smells great.

    a) attic   b) basement   e) playroom
    c) kitchen   d) bedroom

Once you read past the blank you can tell that **c**, kitchen is the answer.

Here are some examples of how the sentence that follows the blank can change the answer:

7. The ball was _____. It was neither too large nor too small.

    a) round   b) square   e) tiny
    c) big   d) little

Only **a**, round would fit.

8. The ball was _____. It was so large, in fact, that I could hardly hold on to it.

    a) round   b) square   e) thin
    c) big   d) little

The answer would be **c**, big.

9. The ball was _____. It was so tiny I could hardly see it.

    a) round   b) square   e) huge
    c) big   d) little

The answer would be **d**, little.

Here is an example of the kind of passage and multiple-choice questions that you might find in the Degrees of Reading Power® section of the CMT 4. The answers have been filled in for you.

Animals have babies just like people have babies. Animal babies, however, grow and act differently than human babies.

When lions have babies, they are called cubs. The lion cubs are ____**1**____ by their mother for the first three months of their lives. After three months, the lion cubs eat the meat that other lions in their family collect. Lion cubs are very active and love to play. The cubs play with each other to get the ____**2**____ they need to grow stronger.

A horse's babies are called fillies and colts. Fillies are the young female horses and colts are the young male horses. Fillies and colts grow very ____**3**____. They need a lot of food to give them energy for so much fast growing. Some young horses can drink up to three gallons of milk a day! When horses are three or four years old, they are adults and can be trained by humans.

1 ○ watched   ○ moved
   ○ washed   ● fed
      ○ met

HINT: To fill in this blank with the correct word, you have to look at the words in the next sentence. The next sentence says, "After three months, the lion cubs eat the meat that other lions in their family collect." The sentence is discussing how the lion cubs eat. The sentence with the blank says, "The lion cubs are _____ by their mother for the first three months of their lives." You need to choose the answer choice that has to do with eating. "Fed" is the best answer.

2 ○ vitamins   ○ weight
   ○ time   ● exercise
      ○ nutrition

HINT: To choose the right word in blank 2, you need to look at the words around this word. The sentence says that lion cubs play with each other to get something they need to get stronger. The previous sentence says that lion cubs are very active. Which of the answer choices is something that cubs would get from playing with each other and that they would need in order to grow stronger? "Exercise" fits best.

3 ● quickly   ○ nicely
   ○ happily   ○ slowly
      ○ easily

HINT: The words in the sentence with the blank will help you figure out the correct answer. This sentence says, "Fillies and colts grow very _____. The next sentence states "They need a lot of food to give them energy for so much fast growing." The word "fast" is a clue. You need to choose a word that means the same as fast. "Quickly" is a good answer. It makes sense in the sentence and means about the same as "fast."

Now try it yourself with the passages on the following pages.

viii

TRAVEL ON WATER

There are many ways to travel on water. You can travel in a boat. You can also water-ski, jet ski or ___1___ on the water.

There are many different kinds of boats. One type of a large boat is called a ship. Ships are used for many reasons. Some ships are used to fight wars as part of the Navy. The largest Navy ship is an aircraft carrier.

Another type of large boat is called a freighter. Freighters are large boats that carry things like cars, steel, and oil. The biggest ocean freighters are oil tankers. Oil tankers carry large containers of oil across the ocean.

There are boats used for business. One business that uses boats is fishing. Fishing boats come in all sizes, from big trawlers to ___2___ lobster boats. Commercial fisherman use fishing boats to travel out onto the water to catch fish that they will then ___3___.

Sometimes boats are used just for fun. These are called pleasure boats. Pleasure boats are very popular among people who love to be on the open water. These boats can ___4___ in size from big yachts to little motorboats. Some pleasure boats do not have motors at all, such as sailboats. Sailboats use the___5___to move. However, some sailboats do have motors on board in case there is no breeze.

There are boats used for sports and exercise. These include rafts, rowboats, canoes, sculls and kayaks. People have sports competitions in sculls and kayaks. These types of boats are good for building strong ___6___ in a person's arm and legs. Some people like to go on rafts or kayaks in rough water, called white water. They find it can be very ___7___.

1 a) float   b) dine
   c) surf   d) glide
      e) bounce

2 a) heavy   b) sharp
   c) tall   d) strong
      e) tiny
3 a) sell   b) cook
   c) release   d) fry
      e) adopt

4 a) grow   b) vary
   c) shrink   d) develop
      e) appear
5 a) sun   b) moon
   c) wind   d) stars
      e) waves

6 a) muscles   b) lines
   c) brains   d) spirits
      e) competitions
7 a) unpleasant   b) disturbing
   c) boring   d) exciting
      e) calming

NEW HAVEN'S EARLY YEARS

On April 24, 1638, a group of five hundred English Puritans sailed into New Haven harbor. The group was ____1____ by the Reverend John Davenport and a wealthy London merchant named Theophilus Eaton. The group soon discovered that the native Quinnipiacks were ____2____ about tribes from neighboring areas raiding their land. It was for this reason that leaders from the Quinnipiacks tribe and other tribes agreed to sell the land to the Puritans. In return, the settlers pledged to ____3____ the local natives. The settlers also agreed to allow them the use of the lands on the east side of the harbor.

New Haven's founders hoped to create a perfect Christian community. They also hoped to start a company in New Haven. They realized that New Haven's large harbor would allow them to trade goods with other towns. They decided that the New Haven harbor would be a good place to start their ____4____.

By 1640, a government had been established. The settlement, originally called Quinnipiac, was renamed New Haven. The town plan was based on a grid of nine squares. This followed the way old English towns were ____5____. At the center of New Haven was a square. This square was called the Greens. It was the public square and the heart of the town. By 1641 New Haven had grown into a community of approximately 800.

Over the next few years, however, the flow of newcomers began to weaken. Trade with the outside world began to shift more towards Boston than New Haven. Puritan leaders in New Haven decided to try and trade directly with England. They were able to fill a ____6____ with materials to sail and sell to England. The ship became known as the "Great Shippe." It set sail in January 1646. However, after setting sail the ship and its crew were never heard from again. This ____7____ ended the dream of creating a trading empire in New Haven. Over the years New Haven became overshadowed by New Amsterdam (New York) and Boston.

1 a) misled   b) served
    c) led   d) paid
      e) named

2 a) happy   b) confused
    c) pleased   d) surprised
      e) upset

3 a) feed   b) protect
    c) attack   d) like
      e) adopt

4 a) business   b) lives
    c) store   d) harbor
      e) army

5 a) ruled   b) imagined
    c) destructed   d) designed
      e) pictured

6 a) car   b) airplane
    c) boat   d) train
      e) truck

7 a) excitement   b) success
    c) trade   d) crew
      e) disaster

HISTORY

We know a lot of history because people ____1____ things down. Some of it we know because of what we have dug up!

You can learn a lot about people by looking at what is left behind after they are gone. You can see what they ate, and what kinds of __2__ they lived in. You can learn about the __3__ they used and the art they created. You can understand what crops they grew. You can even discover which animals they kept as pets and which animals they ____4____.

The most exciting things to dig up are very old writings. Sometimes old writings are only a few words or __5__. They can be found on a stone or a piece of pottery. Some writings are also found on clay tablets. A collection of clay tablet writings were found in a place called Ebla. Ebla was a castle that had ____6____ down. The fire had hardened the clay on the tablets and preserved it for over 3,000 years.

Writing can be discovered in many places. Writings have been discovered in tombs, old forts, and castles. Some have even been found in caves. They are usually found in places where people used to live.

In fact, the biggest find in recent history was in a number of caves. Scientists found scrolls there that were written over 2,000 years ago. These scrolls are called the Dead Sea Scrolls.

The study of the remains of old civilizations is called "archaeology." You probably enjoyed ____7____ in the dirt when you were little, but you probably never thought it was a career you could pursue as an adult!

1 a) told   b) laid
   c) wrote   d) held
        e) threw

2 a) parks   b) boats
   c) cars   d) steel
        e) homes

3 a) roads   b) tools
   c) cars   d) phones
        e) trains

4 a) loved   b) milked
   c) feared   d) harvested
        e) hunted

5 a) questions   b) letters
   c) chapters   d) maps
        e) stories

6 a) fallen   b) flooded
   c) tumbled   d) burned
        e) slid

7 a) digging   b) building
   c) laying   d) stomping
        e) napping

BATTLE OF THE FROGS

Sometimes history can be fun. This is a true story about an odd event that happened in Connecticut.

It was 1754, the time of the French and Indian War. Some American Indian tribes were teamed-up with the French. They were fighting against the British Colonies, attacking many villages in Connecticut.

Colonel Eliphalet Dyer lived in Windham, in northeastern Connecticut. In those days this area of Connecticut was still the frontier. Colonel Dyer was able to enlist most of the men of Windham to fight in the war. The men that stayed behind were afraid of attacks since no one knew how close the ____1____ was.

Their worst fears seemed to have come true one steamy hot June night. Unearthly screams came from out of the __2__. Brave villagers grabbed __3__ and fired blindly into the night. Some believed that their attackers had finally arrived. Some prayed, others hid under their ____4____.

The next morning, people came out of their homes. They could not believe their ____5____. Some people laughed, but most of the people were speechless. They found several hundred dead and dying bullfrogs. The frogs were in a dried-up pond two miles east of the village center. The frogs had made all the ____6____. They had fought each other to the death. They were trying to find water in the dried-up pond.

The story became known all over. Windham became forever known as the scene of the "Battle of the Frogs."

Today a bridge that honors the Battle of the Frogs stands near the site. "The Frog Bridge" has statues of large frogs on each side. Many of the people that ____7____ the bridge each day probably have no idea why it is decorated with such huge frogs!

1 a) enemy   b) city
   c) daytime   d) battleship
          e) winter
2 a) way   b) darkness
   c) radio   d) speaker
          e) mouth
3 a) bottles   b) bats
   c) cans   d) rifles
          e) banisters
4 a) coats   b) breath
   c) bridges   d) hats
          e) beds
5 a) ears   b) friends
   c) noses   d) eyes
          e) stories
6 a) noise   b) mess
   c) food   d) jokes
          e) deals

7 a) build   b) cross
   c) avoid   d) design
          e) paint

4

PHYSICAL ACTIVITY

America has a huge problem called "obesity." Obesity means "being overweight."

One way to prevent becoming overweight is to be more active and move around more. Too much ____1____ is not good for you. Spending too much time watching television or playing video games is also not good for you.

Here are five great ____2____ to help you get active and stay physically fit.

- Find ____3____ during the day when you can be active. Get outside and play even if it is for as little as 10 minutes a day.

- During the commercial breaks of your favorite TV show ____4____ up and do jumping jacks. See how many you can do during one full commercial break.

- Be creative! Think about times during the day when you can run instead of walk. During ____5____ see how many times you can run around the playground. Challenge yourself to run more and more each day.

- Be part of a team! Joining a team sport is a great way to stay active and have fun. Sports like basketball, swimming, softball, and even kickball get your heart rate up and help you stay physically fit. Joining a team is also a great way to create new ____6____.

- Let loose! Go into your room, shut the door and turn on your favorite song. Get those feet moving and ____7____ away.

1 a) running   b) sitting
   c) racing   d) sweating
       e) activity

2 a) coaches   b) places
   c) connections   d) invitations
       e) suggestions

3 a) time   b) light
   c) friends   d) sunlight
       e) excuses

4 a) sit   b) give
   c) make   d) break
       e) stand

5 a) math   b) science
   c) recess   d) library
       e) homeroom

6 a) music   b) friendships
   c) recipes   d) dishes
       e) characters

7 a) write   b) swim
   c) dance   d) read
       e) throw

BEARS IN CONNECTICUT

A few years ago there were no bears in most of Connecticut. At least, they were rarely ever ____1____. Today things are different. Black bear sightings in Connecticut are on the rise.

Bears are attracted to the garbage, pet food, fruit trees, and birdfeeders around ____2____. People who live in Connecticut need to learn more about bears to reduce the chance of bears becoming a problem at their homes. Bears do not normally hurt humans, so they do not need to be ___3___but they should be respected.

- DO make bird feeders and bird food hard to ____4____. Hang feeders at least 10 feet above the ground. Put them six feet away from tree trunks.

- DON'T feed the birds from late March to November. Bears will be out of hibernation and searching for food during these months.

- DO place garbage cans inside a garage or shed. Add ammonia to the ____5____ so it does not taste good to bears. This will work for raccoons, too.

- DO clean and put grills away after use.

- DON'T feed bears. Bears that get used to finding food near your home may become "problem" bears.

- DON'T leave pet food outside overnight.

- DO make sure a bear knows you are there. Wave your arms if you see a bear while you are ____6____.

- DO keep dogs on a leash and under your control. A roaming dog might be seen as a threat to a bear or to its cubs.

- DON'T cook food near your tent or store food inside your tent. Instead, keep food in a secure container or use ____7____ to suspend it between two trees.

1
a) eaten b) missed
c) seen d) bitten
e) raised

2
a) houses b) cars
c) restaurants d) caves
e) gardens

3
a) found b) feared
c) freed d) fed
e) loved

4
a) understand b) reach
c) break d) build
e) read

5
a) feed b) ground
c) garages d) trash
e) cleaning

6
a) baking b) sleeping
c) racing d) hiking
e) sailing

7
a) rope b) elevators
c) magnets d) magic
e) rules

6

LIBRARIES

What do you do when you go to a library? Do you read? Do you study? Do you use a computer? What do you take home from the library?

Libraries have been around for a long time, but your local library today is much different than libraries from the past.

The __1__ libraries were built thousands of years ago. These early libraries just had books about science. These days you can find many different types of books at the library, like biographies, fiction, poetry and more.

Libraries used to be a collection of works in print, but it's not just print anymore. Libraries have now become media centers filled with all types of information. Libraries today __2__ CDs, videos, DVDs and audiobooks. In some libraries, you can even borrow works of art.

While you can take most things out of a library, libraries have reference sections filled with materials that you are not __3__ to borrow, like encyclopedias, magazines, newspapers and almanacs. Usually these materials must __4__ in the library so everyone can use them.

Even the way people search for materials in libraries has __5__ over the years. People used to look up books in card catalogues. Now, many libraries have information stored in computers or even on the Internet. If you want to know what books are stored in the library, all you have to do is look them up on a computer.

In addition to storing information, many libraries today offer programs or __6__ for people who live in the community. They may have a class about nature hiking, or have story time for children. Some libraries may even have movie nights.

Libraries are a great resource for __7__ information and staying connected with the community. They have evolved so much over the years that it is exciting to think of what future libraries will be like.

1 a) largest   b) best
   c) first   d) last
       e) longest

2 a) loan   b) bury
   c) produce   d) clean
       e) shred

3 a) forced   b) asked
   c) demanded   d) allowed
       e) prepared

4 a) live   b) sleep
   c) stay   d) run
       e) form

5 a) thinned   b) changed
   c) remained   d) migrated
       e) worsened

6 a) outings   b) televisions
   c) homes   d) food
       e) activities

7 a) forgetting   b) stealing
   c) hiding   d) gathering
       e) destroying

7

PELÉ

Many people consider Pelé to be the best soccer player to ever play the game.

Pelé was raised in a very poor family. They lived in Brazil. Soccer is very popular there. Many young Brazilians start playing the game at a young age.

Pelé first learned the ____1____ of soccer from his father, who had been a professional soccer player. His father had played the position of center forward. A fractured leg ended his career, but he was happy to teach his son how to play.

Pelé played on the ____2____ of his city. He was able to play on some teams, too. Even as a little boy he was much better than all the other players.

At age 11, he was discovered when one of the best players in Brazil saw him play. This ____3____ player said, "This boy will be the greatest soccer player in the world." He knew right away that Pelé was someone ____4____.

The professional player watched Pelé play for the next four years. He brought Pelé to São Paulo, Brazil, when Pelé was 15. São Paulo is one of the biggest cities in Brazil.

Pelé was soon on a professional team at the age of 16. His skills were ____5____! During his first appearance on the team he scored a goal right away.

From there, his ____6____ continued. In his first league game, he scored four goals. The next season, he was a regular starter. With 32 goals, Pelé was the scoring leader of the São Paulo state league.

Then came the World Cup of 1958. The World Cup is the largest soccer competition in the world. Teams from around the world came to play against each other. Pelé out-shined everyone. People could not believe his incredible ____7____ as he ran down the field.

Pelé played in four World Cups: Sweden 1958, Chile 1962, England 1966, and Mexico 1970. He scored 12 goals in 14 World Cup matches.

1 a) story   b) myth
    c) idea   d) problem
       e) sport

2 a) buildings   b) schools
    c) rivers   d) streets
       e) basements

3 a) horrible   b) strange
    c) awkward   d) excellent
       e) mean

4 a) skinny   b) special
    c) tall   d) famous
       e) average

5 a) lacking   b) funny
    c) impressive   d) slow
       e) boring

6 a) anger   b) teammates
    c) coaching   d) confusion
       e) success

7 a) speed   b) voice
    c) shoes   d) uniform
       e) smile

8

THE HOLE IN THE WALL GANG CAMP

Paul Newman was a famous __1__ who lived in Westport, CT. In the 1970s, he starred in a movie called *Butch Cassidy and the Sundance Kid.* The movie was about bad guys in the Old West. Their __2__ was called "The Hole in the Wall." They were part of "The Hole in the Wall Gang."

In 1988, Paul Newman decided to start a camp for sick kids. He named it "The Hole in the Wall Gang Camp."

The Hole in the Wall Gang Camp is tucked away in northeastern Connecticut, far away from __3__ roads. It sits among high hills, in the middle of __4__ woods.

After you turn off the main road you enter the camp through the camp gates. After entering the gate, a burst of bright colors is the first thing you see. You will then be greeted by __5__ that declare, "Yippee, you're here!"

Across from the camp's lake stand totem poles, tepees and wigwams. There is a boathouse and a gazebo. After you wander down the tree-lined dirt road, past stables, barns and fields, the main building can be seen. The building contains an Olympic-size swimming pool and a theater.

The Hole in Wall Gang Camp has been designed with a Western theme. The OK Corral is the infirmary. Craft-making areas are disguised as Western-style shops. A towering round dining hall is modeled after a Shaker barn.

At this camp, children with cancer or serious blood diseases find __6__, joy and a renewed sense of being kids. They also get to do things they may have not known they were __7__ of doing.

1 a) chef   b) politician
   c) actor   d) doctor
      e) athlete

2 a) hideout   b) cover
   c) leader   d) car
      e) gang

3 a) long   b) brick
   c) busy   d) bumpy
      e) lost

4 a) strange   b) clever
   c) small   d) ugly
      e) thick

5 a) boats   b) signs
   c) animals d) colors
      e) gates

6 a) insects   b) sleep
   c) trouble d) happiness
      e) food

7 a) aware   b) capable
   c) convinced d) tried
      e) bored

ABRAHAM LINCOLN AS A YOUNG MAN

People looked up to Abraham Lincoln for being the 16th president of the United States and for helping to end slavery. But, Abraham Lincoln was also looked up to for another ____1____: he was unusually tall and very strong.

Lincoln reached the ____2____ of six feet four inches when he was young. He was also stronger than most people his age. He could outrun, outlift and outwrestle the other boys. He could chop wood faster, carry a heavier log when building a barn, and top the neighborhood champion in any ____3____ act. He was proud of his strength and speed, but he was more eager to use his mind.

Lincoln felt that the power of using the mind rather than just ____4____ was the key to success. He wanted to not only be stronger than others, but to be able to talk like the preacher, spell like the teacher, argue like the lawyer, and write like the ____5____.

Lincoln didn't think he was better than other people just because he was smart. He was helpful, cheerful and a good listener. When people of all ages came together at community events like corn-huskings or house raisings, Lincoln liked to join in on the fun. He was well-liked and known for his good-nature.

Lincoln's reading skills and excellent memory soon made him the best at telling ____6____ among his friends. He was so skillful at this that people would sit and listen to him for hours, especially children. He would also tell jokes and do funny imitations of energetic preachers and other townspeople. His stories and his wit were playful and never ____7____. He never wanted to hurt the feelings of other people.

Lincoln was funny and smart, as well as tall and strong. He was one of the great leaders of our country.

1 a) time   b) problem
   c) excuse   d) solution
            e) reason
2 a) height   b) weight
   c) scale   d) length
            e) ruler

3 a) drama   b) athletic
   c) long   d) week
            e) exciting

4 a) personality b) looks
   c) muscles   d) brains
            e) anger
5 a) author   b) athlete
   c) policeman   d) criminal
            e) student

6 a) rules   b) lies
   c) mistakes   d) stories
            e) problems

7 a) boring   b) interesting
   c) true   d) false
            e) mean

HOW TO STRETCH

Many people exercise to stay fit and strong. Some people jog or enjoy weight lifting. Some people go to gyms or participate in sports. With all this increased ____1____ comes an increase in injuries.

Injuries can happen if a person does not prepare before exercising. It is smart to develop a warm-up and stretch routine to protect ____2____ and joints.

Stretching should be done before ____3____ activities. It is necessary to lengthen the muscles and tendons that tend to shorten and cramp when they have not been moving. Do not stretch without ____4____ up. A good warm-up helps protect against injuries while stretching.

Does it matter how you stretch? Years ago, people bent over with straight knees to touch their toes. They bounced up and down. They were using gravity to help force the stretch. This type of stretching ended up causing a lot of injuries.

Today, we know that it is best to stretch in slow, controlled movements. Once you have stretched as far as you can without feeling pain, you should hold the position. Pain is a ____5____ that you've stretched too far.

Many trainers also recommend a stretch after exercise. Use it as part of your cool-down. It can help prevent soreness and ____6____ after a workout.

Stretching exercises are not just for athletes. They can help keep anyone's body more flexible and strong. Some people stretch regularly just to keep ____7____.

1 a) excitement   b) pain
   c) activity   d) fun
            e) time

2 a) strength   b) children
   c) muscles   d) arms
            e) legs

3 a) quiet   b) effortless
   c) daytime   d) lazy
            e) difficult

4 a) getting   b) jumping
   c) sitting   d) warming
            e) letting

5 a) limb   b) signal
   c) direction   d) leg
            e) word

6 a) cramps   b) diseases
   c) tripping   d) hunger
            e) mistakes

7 a) healthy   b) tall
   c) injured   d) sore
            e) stiff

NIGHT CRAWLERS

At one time, American worms had the country all to themselves. Then ____1____ arrived.

No one knows for sure how the first European worms came to America from Europe. It is believed they most likely came with the settlers, hiding in ships, seed stock and potted plants.

Once in the New World these "stowaway" worms adapted to the new ____2____. They enjoyed the new soils, climate and plant life and began to spread. In fact, ____3____ who study worms believe the European worms may have pushed out native worms from the best food and soils.

One modern-day relative of European worms is called the night crawler. Night crawlers are among the country's largest worms, reaching eight inches or more in length. They are widespread throughout North America today.

Night crawlers are also really ____4____. You've probably discovered this if you've tried to nab one peeking out of its hole. Night crawlers spend a lot of their time on the soil surface getting snacks. Their ____5____ is important in helping them escape watchful birds and other hungry predators.

Night crawlers are important to agriculture. They help mix ____6____ and make more nutrient-rich food for plants. Scientists don't know if bigger worms do this any better than smaller worms.

If strange worms had not invaded would our plants have grown as well? We don't really know for sure. One thing we do know: If you're going fishing, a ____7____, juicy night crawler is a good worm to use.

1 a) deserters   b) invaders
   c) resisters   d) tourists
        e) retreaters

2 a) environment   b) people
   c) ships   d) organism
        e) water

3 a) teachers   b) children
   c) scientists   d) doctors
        e) animals

4 a) slow   b) smart
   c) fast   d) colorful
        e) shiny

5 a) speed   b) sight
   c) color   d) size
        e) smell

6 a) water   b) grass
   c) drinks   d) medicine
        e) soil

7 a) sour   b) plump
   c) chewy   d) lean
        e) sick

12

CABOOSE

The word "caboose" is from the Dutch language. It means the "galley of a ship". More modern terms for caboose include "crummy," "cabin," and "hack". In English, a caboose is a part of a train.

A caboose is the final car on a train. It used to be an office for the conductor of the train. The conductor was responsible for the train. That meant that the conductor had a lot of ____1____ to do. He was responsible for keeping track of a lot of records on paper. Some records he kept track of were the number of cars on the train, and the times and ____2____ the train made its stops.

Normally, train crews would be scheduled to work for two days straight. Sometimes they might work for as long as a week straight because of bad ____3____ or other types of delays. This was hard because the trains did not have a place for the crew members to lay down. By 1850, the new design of the cars included ____4____. This made crew members very ____5____. They could finally lay their heads down on a pillow during long train rides.

It was necessary for the crews to watch the train carefully. They watched for any type of problems on the outside of the train. They were watching for hot wheel bearings, dragging car parts, or any parts sticking out. The best ____6____ the crew members had was from the top of the train. So, a lookout, or cupola, was added to the top of the caboose.

By the 1920's, the caboose was made completely out of steel. Steel was used because it was fire-resistant and it could withstand the pushing, hitting and pulling by the much larger locomotives connected to the caboose. Cabooses suffered from extremely ____7____ motions when long freight trains started and stopped. Every caboose had an overhead grab bar to keep crew members safe.

Modern freight cars became so tall that other trains could not be "eyeballed" from the cupola. Cabooses were re-designed with the viewing windows on their sides. These windows allowed crew members to see on-coming trains. Today, crew members ride in large, comfortable cars on the train. Unlike old trains the last car is no longer a caboose.

1 a) homework   b) paperwork
  c) lifting   d) packing
        e) driving
2 a) ways   b) reason
  c) years   d) places
        e) decades

3 a) weather   b) food
  c) ideas   d) bosses
        e) pay
4 a) pictures   b) bathrooms
  c) beds   d) books
        e) kitchens
5 a) angry   b) happy
  c) sad   d) concerned
        e) upset

6 a) view   b) meal
  c) sleep   d) play
        e) strike

7 a) slow   b) long
  c) smooth   d) jerky
        e) fast

13

LEATHERBACK TURTLES

The leatherback sea turtle weighs 650 to 1,200 ___1___. These turtles usually grow to be five to six feet long. The record length is nine feet. The leatherback turtle's flipper span is ___2___. On a seven-foot turtle the flipper span is about nine feet!

The leatherback can live for a very long time. Most are alive for 50 years or more. Leatherbacks mainly eat jellyfish. They also ___3___ on sea urchin, crustaceans, squid, fish and floating seaweed.

The leatherback has a smooth shell. It is hard and covered with skin. The top shell is dark brown or black, while the bottom shell is mostly white. Irregular patches of white may appear almost anywhere on the sea turtle.

The limbs of the leatherback sea turtle are black. They look like paddles. They use these paddles to ___4___ through the water. Leatherbacks have no claws. Young leatherbacks are black, and they often have more white markings than adults do.

This type of turtle can live in many different types of ___5___. It can be found in the hot tropical Atlantic, Pacific and Indian Oceans and the Mediterranean Sea. It can be found as far north as the chilly British Isles and as far south as Australia. In the United States, the species lives mainly along the sunny Florida coast.

Leatherbacks mate offshore in shallow waters. The females make their ___6___ out of sticks and sand from the beaches. They make them at night. These become the place where the females lay their eggs.

The females usually lay 80–85 eggs each. When the hatchlings break out of their eggs, they are about three inches big. The ___7___ turtles then head straight towards the ocean to enjoy their first swim.

1 a) inches   b) pounds
   c) grains   d) meters
           e) times
2 a) surprising   b) skinny
   c) enormous   d) scary
           e) tall

3 a) rest   b) balance
   c) perch   d) spy
           e) feed

4 a) glide   b) climb
   c) chop   d) whack
           e) whisper

5 a) plants   b) pools
   c) grass   d) climates
           e) shelters

6 a) living   b) meals
   c) drinks   d) bridges
           e) nests

7 a) heavy   b) large
   c) baby   d) slimy
           e) few

14

TRUMBULL LITTLE LEAGUE

The baseball Little League World Series takes place every August in South Williamsport, PA. In 1989, a certain Little League team made the state of Connecticut proud. That team, of course, was Trumbull, Connecticut—the 1989 Little League World ___1___.

The team's amazing run of ___2___ over all of the other teams brought the town of Trumbull into the national spotlight. Thanks to this team of young baseball players, Americans could see that Trumbull was a special place to live, with a strong focus on family. The town's ___3___ was shown best when 15,000 people jammed into the streets to honor their hometown heros.

What memories the team must have. They can probably still hear the crowd ___4___, "USA! USA!"

Why wouldn't they have been proud? They had an incredible team. Like Dan McGrath, whose perfect throw to home plate stopped a Taiwan player from scoring. And Andy Paul, whose incredible home run against Davenport, Iowa is probably still in outer space somewhere! It was the ___5___ of all 15 players that led the team to victory.

Now, nearly 20 years later, one player in particular is still making Trumbull proud, Chris Drury. As pitcher in the championship game, Drury only let two runs score. He was also very important in ___6___ Taipei, Taiwan. The win against Taipei, Taiwan led to the team's championship. Today, Chris Drury is a professional hockey player for the New York Rangers. He is one of the top players in the National Hockey League.

Chris always makes time for his fans. Especially his fans from Connecticut. Chris says that he will never ___7___ where he came from—the great town of Trumbull, Connecticut.

1 a) Champions   b) Competitors
     c) Organizers   d) Fans
        e) Parents

2 a) uniforms   b) skills
     c) coaches   d) victories
        e) pictures

3 a) mayor   b) mall
     c) pride   d) food
        e) sadness

4 a) gasping   b) chanting
     c) waving   d) laughing
        e) whispering

5 a) friends   b) towns
     c) names   d) teamwork
        e) coaches

6 a) defeating   b) helping
     c) comforting   d) scoring
        e) pushing

7 a) like   b) represent
     c) enjoy   d) leave
        e) forget

MICHAEL JORDAN

Many people consider Michael Jordan to be the __1__ basketball player of all time. He could score baskets from anywhere on the court. When he __2__, he seemed to fly in the air. He had great body control. His dunks were creative, awesome and historic.

While leading all scorers in the National Basketball Association (NBA), for many years Michael Jordan was chosen as the defensive player of the year. Think of it: the best offensive player, scoring lots of points, and defensive player, keeping other players from scoring.

Michael's most __3__ shot was known as the "fall-away jumper." Instead of jumping straight towards the basket, in this well-known shot he would fall away from the basket while shooting. He was extremely tough to guard. He was fast and tricky and had great moves. He was taller than most other guards. His hands were __4__, and his arms were long. This made it __5__ for him to hold the basketball in one hand and keep it away from other players.

When Michael Jordan stopped playing basketball for the first time in 1993, he went out with a bang. At that __6__ game, he made an incredible shot with time running out and won a world championship. He attempted a career in baseball. He played on a minor league team for a while, but he rejoined his basketball team, the Chicago Bulls in 1995. He led them to three more championships: 1996, 1997, and 1998.

Michael stopped playing for a second time in 1999, but once again, his love of the game was too __7__ to keep him away. He returned to the NBA as a member of the Washington Wizards in September 2001. He played for the team for two seasons before he officially stopped in April 2003 at the age of 40.

Michael Jordan holds the NBA record for highest career regular season scoring average with 30.1 points per game, as well as averaging a record 33.4 points per game in the playoffs.

1 a) slowest   b) meanest
     c) shortest   d) strangest
        e) greatest

2 a) ran   b) threw
     c) jumped   d) fell
        e) yawned

3 a) strange   b) famous
     c) lucky   d) noisy
        e) recent

4 a) huge   b) ordinary
     c) tight   d) average
        e) insignificant

5 a) difficult   b) impossible
     c) easy   d) healthy
        e) unlikely

6 a) final   b) second
     c) initial   d) boring
        e) first

7 a) silly   b) strong
     c) confusing   d) angry
        e) fake

TRAFFIC IN CONNECTICUT

There is often too much traffic on our highways. For example, a trip from Bridgeport to Stamford will take 20 minutes with no cars on the road. The ____1____ trip will take over 60 minutes during rush hour.

Something has to be done. No one likes to spend that much time driving to work. Driving home is even worse.

People will avoid taking ____2____ if it takes so long to get to work. This is not good for Connecticut.

The problem is that no one is sure what the solution is. Connecticut cannot build more highways. There is no room. Also, the state does not have enough ____3____ for such a large project.

Many people believe that the answer is to get more people to use mass transportation, such as trains and ____4____. The problem with that solution is that there is not enough parking at the train stations. We can build new train stations with lots of parking, but the trains are already too ____5____. There is no money to buy more trains.

Another problem is the amount of huge trucks on the highways. What can we do about the trucks? Trucks are big. When trucks go too fast, they can be ____6____, causing accidents on the road. Since there are so many trucks on the road, they can make the traffic worse.

Some think the answer is to use freight trains in place of the trucks, since freight trains can carry cargo just like trucks do. However, it is hard for freight trains to get to Connecticut because a new bridge is needed. But even if the bridge were built, these trains would not solve the traffic problem. The cargo would have to be loaded and unloaded onto trucks which would then travel on the highway.

Some people think building a bridge across Long Island Sound might help. It would connect land in Connecticut and New York.

Without some type of major change, traffic will ____7____ a problem for the rest of our lives.

1 a) other   b) faster
   c) same   d) daily
          e) exciting

2 a) classes   b) jobs
   c) walks   d) rides
          e) vacations

3 a) paint   b) paper
   c) metal   d) money
          e) tools

4 a) buses   b) planes
   c) telephones   d) elevators
          e) submarines

5 a) empty   b) crowded
   c) old   d) attractive
          e) heavy

6 a) colorful   b) slow
   c) small   d) loud
          e) dangerous

7 a) remove   b) occupy
   c) remain   d) become
          e) reserve

17

STAMP COLLECTING

Since they were invented, people have taken an interest in stamps. They have been used to mail letters for over 200 years. The oldest and ___1___ stamps are the most valuable.

You can collect stamps for free, they come on your mail. To detach the stamp from the letters, put the letter in warm water and let it ___2___. The stamp will just float off. Then let the stamp dry.

Keep your stamps in an envelope. At some point you may want to ___3___ an album for your stamps. That is what many collectors do.

If you know adults who have businesses, they may get mail from other countries. They may have stamps from as far away as Mexico, Poland, or Australia. If you ask them, they may let you have those stamps, which would broaden your stamp collection.

Through stamps, you can learn a lot about the world. Every country has its own stamps. The U.S. has printed stamps representing every American ___4___. You can learn a lot of geography from stamps.

Many countries put some type of history on their stamps. Some country's stamps have kings and ___5___. Each of America's presidents are on stamps. You can learn a lot of history from stamps.

Most stamps include the name of the country and the __6__ of the stamp. Many stamps have words in the country's native language. If you study these stamps enough, you could learn some new words and phrases.

Many stamps are pretty, showing flowers or animals. Others have ___7___ people, like athletes, artists, writers and movie stars. Some even have fictional people and cartoon characters on them.

Some people collect stamps from only one country. Others collect stamps from around the world.

1 a) ugliest   b) worst
  c) rarest   d) darkest
    e) heaviest

2 a) dissolve   b) dry
  c) fade   d) rip
    e) soak

3 a) make   b) hold
  c) sell   d) throw
    e) save

4 a) person   b) town
  c) state   d) dollar
    e) pledge

5 a) doctors   b) trees
  c) birds   d) nurses
    e) queens

6 a) height   b) volume
  c) model   d) planet
    e) price

7 a) young   b) famous
  c) strange   d) funny
    e) boring

18

A BRIEF HISTORY OF THE MARITIME AQUARIUM

In the mid-1970s, officials were looking for a way make South Norwalk a more popular place to visit. They finally came up with plans for a major local attraction. Everyone hoped that this new attraction would bring both ___1___ and money to the historic area of South Norwalk.

A new maritime center was planned. It was to include an aquarium featuring live ___2___ from Long Island Sound, including sharks, dolphins, and other types of fish. They also planned on building an IMAX movie theatre. It would have a ___3___ eight stories wide and six stories high.

In 1986, ground-breaking ceremonies took place on the site of an abandoned brick building. It had been an 1860s iron works ___4___. The big building was on the South Norwalk waterfront.

The Maritime Aquarium has been at the center of a major ___5___ in South Norwalk. The area now bustles by day with people visiting its unique shops, boutiques, and coffee shops. At night its nightclubs and restaurants draw crowds as well.

Each year, over 500,000 visitors come to the Aquarium. That makes it one of the ___6___ attractions in Connecticut. Among the Aquarium's visitors are more than 150,000 schoolchildren on field trips.

In 2005, the Maritime Aquarium started promoting a new vision. The Aquarium now focuses on teaching those who come to visit about preserving and ___7___ Long Island Sound and the animals that live there.

1 a) animals   b) people
   c) coins   d) products
     e) babies

2 a) water   b) rocks
   c) wildlife   d) plants
     e) performers

3 a) door   b) seat
   c) screen   d) tank
     e) stage

4 a) factory   b) farm
   c) mine   d) kitchen
     e) restaurant

5 a) rule   b) problem
   c) project   d) square
     e) turnaround

6 a) oldest   b) closest
   c) tallest   d) strangest
     e) largest

7 a) avoiding   b) hiding
   c) trashing   d) protecting
     e) littering

HOW COLUMBUS GOT HIS IDEA

When Christopher Columbus was at school he __1__ about a certain man named Pythagoras. Pythagoras had lived in Greece thousands of years before Columbus was born. Pythagoras had said that the earth was round "like a ball or an orange." As Columbus grew older he made maps and studied the sea, and read books. He listened to what other people said. He began to believe that this man named Pythagoras might be correct, and that the earth was round, though everybody declared it was ___2___.

"If it is round," he said to himself, "what is the use of trying to sail around Africa to get to China? Why not just sail west and keep going right around the world until you strike China? I believe it could be done," said Columbus.

By this time Columbus was a man. He was thirty years old and was a great ___3___. He had been the captain of a number of ships. He had sailed north and south and east. Although people respected him, when he said that the earth was round, everyone laughed at him and said that he was ___4___.

"Why, how can the earth be round?" they cried. "The __5__ would all spill out if it were, and the men who live on the other side of the world would all be standing on their heads with their __6__ waving in the air." And then they laughed at him even more.

But Columbus did not think that this idea was anything to laugh at. He believed it so strongly and felt so sure that he was __7__, that he set out to find someone who would give him ships and crewmen and money. He needed these because he wanted to try something no one had done before. He wanted to try to find a way to China by sailing out into the West and across the Atlantic Ocean.

1. a) joked   b) screamed
   c) learned   d) dreamed
       e) argued

2. a) hollow   b) flat
   c) hot   d) cold
       e) old

3. a) sailor   b) teacher
   c) singer   d) artist
       e) chef

4. a) angry   b) mean
   c) excited   d) smart
       e) crazy

5. a) mountains   b) clouds
   c) words   d) water
       e) truth

6. a) teeth   b) heads
   c) hands   d) feet
       e) hats

7. a) right   b) strange
   c) dumb   d) mistaken
       e) angry

20

VINLAND

One of the first settlers of Greenland was a man named Heriolf. When he came to the country, he was without his son, Biarni Heriolfson. Biarni was in Iceland at the time. When he was sailing to join his father in Greenland, he was __1__ off-course and discovered an unknown land.

Years later, Leif Ericson, a fellow explorer and Viking, asked Biarni about his voyage. Leif followed Biarni's course. He found and explored the coast of what is now known as Canada.

Ericson then sailed south and discovered a new __2__. It was totally surrounded by water on all sides. It was present-day Newfoundland. He named it "Vinland," because he found grape vines there. Leif stayed for the winter. He returned to Greenland in the __3__, when it was much warmer.

Leif had a brother named Thorvald. Thorvald also wanted to become an explorer and find new lands. He borrowed a ship and set out to __4__ "Vinland the Good." He spent the winter there. In the summer he did more discovering.

One day Thorvald saw three canoes. Under the canoes were nine "Skraelings." That is what they called the Native Americans. The Vikings killed eight of them but one __5__. The next day many more Skraelings returned with bows and arrows. The Vikings used their shields. Most of them were able to avoid the arrows. One person was hit, however. That was Thorvald.

As he was dying, Thorvald asked to be buried in a place he had liked. He became the first Viking to be buried in North America.

Thorvald and Leif had a __6__ named Freydis. She came to Vinland after her brothers. While there, natives attacked the Viking settlers once again. The men were all __7__ and started to run away. However, Freydis picked up a sword and charged at the natives. She killed some and scared the rest away.

1 a) arriving   b) blown
   c) sleeping   d) shaken
            e) standing

2 a) island   b) rock
   c) water   d) explorer
            e) planet

3 a) snow   b) fall
   c) spring   d) water
            e) night

4 a) ride   b) walk
   c) harvest   d) inspect
            e) destroy

5 a) fought   b) died
   c) escaped   d) screamed
            e) left

6 a) cousin   b) uncle
   c) mother   d) friend
            e) sister

7 a) excited   b) frightened
   c) amazed   d) pleased
            e) interested

PACIFIC GRAY WHALES

Female gray whales are very large. They can be up to 45 feet long and weigh as much as 70,000 pounds. Males are slightly smaller. Baby whales, or calves, are about 15 feet long at birth.

Gray whales spend the ___1___ in the Arctic Ocean, when it is warm outside. However, they ___2___ to warmer waters during the winter. The whales travel along the coast of the United States and Mexico. Each of their trips can be as long as 6,000 miles.

___3___ females travel to lagoons to give birth. They often stay to raise their calves. They come to the lagoons because they are usually protected from ocean currents and predators.

Gray whales are "benthic" feeders. That means they search for food on the ___4___ of the ocean. They eat tiny shrimp-like animals that live on the ocean floor. Gray whales are baleen whales. Baleen whales do not have teeth. They have plates of baleen that hang from the upper jaw. These plates are used to ___5___ food from the water.

In the past, whales were hunted for their baleen. Before we had plastic, baleen was used to make combs and even buggy whips. Some cultures still hunt whales. However, this type of hunting is regulated. It does not affect the whale population as a whole.

Have you ever heard of "friendly whales?" This term usually refers to the gray whales. In the lagoons of Mexico, gray whales sometimes ___6___ small boats. It seems like whales are interested in these boats or, perhaps, the people inside. Sometimes they get close enough to allow delighted passengers a chance to reach out and touch them. Scientists are not sure why the whales in the lagoons do this. Most wild animals are too ___7___ either to get close to people or to allow people to get close to them in this way.

1 a) cold   b) year
   c) winter   d) summer
     e) week

2 a) move   b) look
   c) remain   d) sink
     e) jump

3 a) Smart   b) Brave
   c) Pregnant   d) Wise
     e) Injured

4 a) peak   b) bottom
   c) middle   d) waves
     e) top

5 a) keep   b) bond
   c) melt   d) destroy
     e) separate

6 a) eat   b) approach
   c) attack   d) block
     e) disturb

7 a) tired   b) active
   c) nice   d) shy
     e) happy

22

CONNECTICUT INDUSTRY

Connecticut is often described as the "Arsenal of the Nation." It gained this reputation as early as the American Revolution. Early in the 19th century, Eli Whitney and Simeon North began making Connecticut weapons with interchangeable ____1____. This is generally recognized as the beginning of modern mass production.

Colt in Hartford, Remington Arms in Bridgeport and Winchester in New Haven were just some of the top gun and rifle ____2____ in Connecticut.

Waterbury became the "Brass City." Danbury was the "Hat City." Willimantic was the "Thread City." Bridgeport was ____3____ as the industrial capital of Connecticut.

New Haven's economy grew during the Civil War era. The city's carriage industry became one of the nation's largest for many years. New Haven also produced rubber goods, clocks, pianos and a wide ____4____ of other products.

Immigrant workers later ____5____ New Haven to become a leading producer of clocks, plows, wagons, and clothing.

Through the years, Connecticut has given the world such varied ____6____ as vulcanized rubber, friction matches, sewing machines, steamboats, safety fuses, lollipops, cork screws, mechanical calculators, cylindrical locks and the submarine.

Today, Connecticut's manufacturing industry continues to be highly diversified. Jet aircraft engines, helicopters and nuclear submarines have continued to make the state a top producer of ____7____ equipment.

1 a) cars   b) parts
    c) tires   d) arms
       e) names

2 a) collectors   b) swingers
    c) hurlers   d) places
       e) makers

3 a) known   b) shown
    c) closed   d) sent
       e) made

4 a) area   b) path
    c) range   d) river
       e) divide

5 a) helped   b) moved
    c) took   d) limited
       e) spread

6 a) scares   b) talents
    c) elements   d) inventions
       e) stores

7 a) food   b) transportation
    c) building   d) clothing
       e) plastic

23

SEALS

Four different types of seals ____1____ through the waters of the Long Island Sound. They are especially active from December through May. They are the gray seal, harbor seal, harp seal and hooded seal.

The gray seal is seven to eight feet long and weighs up to 800 pounds. It has a long, horse-like face. It can range in ____2____ from nearly white to dark brown or even black with a blotchy patterning.

The harbor seal is five to six feet long. It weighs up to 220 pounds. It has a short muzzle. It is light gray, tan or brown with dark spots on its back.

The harp seal would usually only be seen as a young animal. It would be about three feet long, weigh up to 75 pounds, and have a short muzzle. It is gray to dark tan with dark brown spots and has claws on its front ____3____.

The hooded seal would also likely be seen as a young seal. It would be about three feet long and weigh up to 90 pounds. It would have a steel-blue colored pelt with a light underbelly but no spots. It also would have claws on its front flippers.

Seals on a ____4____ have usually only come out of the water to rest. They are interesting animals. They are often quite ____5____, especially the young ones. Remember, though, that they are still wild animals. They may bite if you walk over to get a better look. Enjoy watching them from a distance. Keep pets away, too.

If you ____6____ the seal might have a health problem, the experts to call are found at Mystic Marine Aquarium. They will respond to calls about sick or ____7____ marine animals along the coast of Connecticut and Rhode Island. The aquarium also monitors local seal populations.

1 a) talk   b) walk
   c) break   d) travel
        e) shine

2 a) weight   b) size
   c) height   d) life
        e) color

3 a) nose   b) beak
   c) flippers   d) mask
        e) teeth

4 a) boat   b) beach
   c) coat   d) coin
        e) bench
5 a) cute   b) ill
   c) dangerous   d) scary
        e) talkative

6 a) hope   b) forget
   c) dream   d) think
        e) learn
7 a) ugly   b) upset
   c) angry   d) broken
        e) injured

24

COVERED BRIDGES

New England is ____1____ for its covered bridges. Vermont and New Hampshire each have dozens of these unique ____2____. Connecticut does not have quite as many. But they can still be found here.

Litchfield County in the northwestern part of the state has the most covered bridges. Perhaps the nicest covered bridge in the state is the West Cornwall Covered Bridge. This ___3___, red-painted bridge was built in 1841 and has been in service since 1864. You can still drive across the bridge. It ___4___ the Housatonic River for a distance of 242 feet.

To reach the West Cornwall Covered Bridge, take Route 7 to where it ____5____ Route 128 in West Cornwall. Turn onto Route 128 East. You will drive right across the covered bridge. Stop for a while in West Cornwall. It is a beautiful little town.

Travel just a bit farther south of West Cornwall on Route 7. You will find two more covered bridges. The first is in Kent Falls State Park. Built in 1974, Kent Falls Covered Bridge is just a ___6___ footpath. It is only 37 feet long. It is a lovely spot to visit and photograph. It is best seen in the fall.

If you continue south on Route 7, you will come to the Bulls Bridge on your right. This covered bridge crosses the Housatonic River. It continues to carry _____7_____ leaving Connecticut for nearby New York State. It was built in 1842.

Hartford County has one covered bridge. It is in a park in the town of Avon. It is called Huckleberry Hill Bridge. This 35-foot bridge was built in 1968.

1 a) unknown   b) hated
   c) famous   d) forgotten
           e) mistaken
2 a) landforms   b) states
   c) parts   d) structures
           e) names

3 a) modern   b) miniature
   c) secret   d) historic
           e) lonely
4 a) travels   b) spans
   c) disconnects   d) measures
           e) reflects
5 a) leaves   b) breaks
   c) meets   d) destroys
           e) leaps

6 a) narrow   b) long
   c) tall   d) vast
           e) hidden

7 a) water   b) weight
   c) wood   d) trash
           e) traffic

CATS

A kitten's body ____1____ can triple in the first few weeks of life. It can go from 1 to 3 pounds very quickly. It is very important that kittens receive the proper nutrition. They need it so they can grow properly.

As soon as a kitten is adopted, a daily care routine should begin. This process should be fun. It should include treats, play, and a ____2____ voice. As cats age, they will become more tolerant of handling and restraint. That will make it easier to care for them.

Cat mothers are ____3____ and protective of their young. A kitten ____4____ from its mother at too early an age may grow up scared and insecure. Kittens should be eight weeks old before they are taken away from their mother.

Cats are known for their ability to ____5____ for themselves in the wild. However, the average life span of a feral, or wild, cat is only about two years. Household pets rely on people for their care and feeding. They require a lot of attention to live a long healthy life.

Cats like to be warm – the warmer the better. They may curl up over a heat vent, in front of a heater or right in front of the fireplace to sleep. This is ____6____ behavior for a cat.

Cats spend most of the day sleeping. The three types of sleep they experience are brief napping, longer light sleep and deep sleep. Kittens only have deep sleep during their first month of life.

Cats like food to be at room ____7____. Refrigerated food should be warmed briefly in the microwave. Then stir to mix up hot and cold spots. Before you give it to your cat, always check to make sure that the food is not too hot.

1 a) weight   b) spots
   c) height   d) fur
        e) color

2 a) loud   b) sharp
   c) harsh   d) soft
        e) mean

3 a) weak   b) scary
   c) loving   d) uncaring
        e) rude
4 a) born   b) separated
   c) written   d) erased
        e) handled
5 a) fend   b) farm
   c) love   d) cook
        e) crave

6 a) odd   b) silly
   c) rare   d) normal
        e) fun

7 a) temperature   b) level
   c) size   d) rate
        e) smell

26

AMUSEMENT PARKS

Amusement parks have a long history in Connecticut. Many cities and towns had amusement parks long ago. They were favorite places for children to go. Years ago, there were many amusement parks in this state. Unfortunately, there are only two historic parks still ____1____. The oldest amusement park in America is Lake Compounce in Bristol, Connecticut dating back to 1847.

The first carousel opened in 1911 and the electric roller ___2___ came just three years later. Speedboat rides started in 1929. A miniature railroad was installed in 1943. It came from Gillette Castle.

The amusement park Lake Quassapaug opened in Middlebury in 1908. It has not changed much over the years. If you want to see a real ____3____ park, you should visit "Quassy."

Two of the older amusement parks are gone, but not __4__. One was called Pleasure Beach. It was located in Bridgeport, on an island. There was a bridge to connect it to the city. It closed in the 1950s. Today the bridge is broken, making it very difficult to get to Pleasure Island.

Some people believe that the best amusement park in Connecticut was Savin Rock in West Haven. It was famous for its scary fun house. At Savin Rock, kids liked three rides the best. One was a motorboat ride that let you ___5___ your own motorboat along a narrow, winding course. Another was the ___6___ cars. What great fun it was to bounce off your friend's car.

Then there was a carousel. Kids loved going up and down on the beautiful horses and going around and around at what seemed like a great speed. Beautiful ____7____ played from the speaker in the middle. On a lot of carousels there was a pole sticking out with rings at the end. Kids would try to grab a ring as they went by. If you got the brass ring you could get the next ride for free.

Today, school and church fairs remind us of these old amusement parks. The rides and games are a lot like the old parks.

1 a) remembered b) known
   c) closed   d) important
          e) open

2 a) wheel   b) train
   c) coaster   d) cars
          e) skates

3 a) island   b) classic
   c) modern   d) small
          e) expensive

4 a) forgotten   b) built
   c) allowed   d) captured
          e) free

5 a) build   b) create
   c) buy   d) protect
          e) steer

6 a) crash   b) race
   c) bumper   d) water
          e) speed

7 a) fireworks   b) music
   c) lasers   d) dancers
          e) scenes

THE CONSERVATION KIDS' CLUB

Meet Bubba, the green tree frog. He is a froggy friend who oversees the monthly club meetings of the Conservation Kids' Club. He is the club's ____1____. The club is for kids who are six to 13 years of age. They meet at the Runge Conservation Nature Center.

"I've been in the Kids' Club since it started," says Doug Johnson, age 8. "I think the Go Batty program was my favorite. We got to feel a fake bat and see a real one. We even had a bat snack at the 'Bat Buffet.'"

Each month includes a nature-related theme. For each month's nature-related project, even the snack focuses on the nature-related theme. One year a project included Snakes Alive, Otter-mania, and Insect-O-Rama. Experts in the field who are informative and ____2____ speak to the group. Kids' Club members are learning to value the ____3____ world around them.

"I learned that bats are flying mammals and that there's millions of them," ____4____ Allison Yamnitz, age 8. "People make up funny stuff about bats. They say that they're blood suckers and stuff. That isn't true of Missouri bats. I know that isn't true."

The animal world has its own set of rumors to set straight. Jenny Morris ____5____ another truth. She was climbing Towering Oak Trail on the Kids' Club night hike. "I saw an owl. I learned that they can't turn their heads all the way around! It only looks that way. They can just turn it most of the way in both ____6____."

The main reason Conservation Kids' Club was created was to educate kids ____7____ to know more about nature.

The Kids' Club attracted over 250 youngsters at the first meeting. For good reason. It's a free, family-oriented program that lets kids learn about and enjoy nature at the same time.

1 a) sponge   b) toad
  c) mascot   d) founder
      e) friend

2 a) boring   b) distracting
  c) entertaining d) caring
      e) calming

3 a) scary   b) close
  c) fake   d) historical
      e) natural

4 a) questioned b) planned
  c) asked   d) explained
      e) sang

5 a) masked   b) questioned
  c) lost   d) discovered
      e) created

6 a) places   b) directions
  c) times   d) methods
      e) days

7 a) surprised b) forced
  c) embarrassed d) scared
      e) eager

EARTHQUAKES IN CONNECTICUT

There have always been "rumblings" in Connecticut in an area called Moodus. American Indians called the area "Morehemoodus," which means "a place of noises." The town name "Moodus" came from this word. No one knew what caused these ____1____ until scientists figured it out. The earth noises are a unique type of earthquake rumbling.

The most severe earthquake in Connecticut's history occurred on May 16, 1791. It happened in East Haddam, a town next to Moodus. It began at 8 o'clock p.m. when there were two very heavy shocks right after each other. The first was the most powerful.

The earth appeared to have ____2____ shakes. Stone walls were thrown down, chimneys were toppled, and doors which had been latched were thrown open. Afterwards a long crack in the ____3____ was discovered.

A short time later, 30 lighter shocks followed. About 100 more were counted during the night.

The shock was felt from a great ____4____. It was severe 12 miles south in Clinton. A man named Captain Benedict was walking the deck of his ship when he saw fish leaping out of the water. The fish were ____5____ in every direction, as far as his eyes could see.

The next major trembling ____6____ at Hartford in April 1837. It knocked loose articles, set lamps swinging, even rang bells. Alarmed ____7____ rushed from their homes into the streets.

In August 1840, an earthquake of similar strength occurred. It was centered a few miles southwest of the 1837 tremor. It shook Hartford quite strongly and was felt at many points in Connecticut. However, no damage resulted.

1 a) movements   b) motions
   c) problems   d) sounds
      e) lights

2 a) violent   b) peaceful
   c) calm   d) gentle
      e) normal

3 a) ocean   b) clouds
   c) ground   d) air
      e) sky

4 a) place   b) distance
   c) closeness   d) tower
      e) building

5 a) running   b) spitting
   c) walking   d) riding
      e) jumping

6 a) screamed   b) sounded
   c) shuffled   d) ate
      e) happened

7 a) teachers   b) people
   c) animals   d) plants
      e) booths

29

FLOSSING

Flossing is when you use a piece of special string, or floss, to clean between your teeth.

You should floss to reduce the millions of bacteria in your mouth. These tiny creatures feed on the bits of food left on your teeth. They live in plaque, a sticky film left on your teeth after ____1____, which can be removed by flossing.

Brushing your teeth gets rid of some of the bacteria in your mouth. Flossing gets rid of the bacteria hiding in the tiny __2__ between your teeth where your toothbrush can't reach. Brushing without flossing is like washing only __3__ your face. One side gets clean while the other stays __4__.

If you don't floss, you allow plaque to ____5____ between your teeth. Eventually it hardens into tartar. Plaque can be removed by brushing, but only your ____6____ can remove tartar.

How do I floss correctly?

- Break off about 18 inches of floss and wrap most of it around one of your middle fingers.

- Wrap the remaining floss around the same finger of the opposite hand. This finger will move up the floss as it becomes dirty.

- Hold the floss tightly between your thumbs and forefingers. Guide the floss between your teeth using a gentle rubbing motion. Never snap the floss into the gums.

- When the floss reaches the gumline, curve it into a C shape against one tooth.

- Gently slide it into the area between the gum and the tooth. Hold the floss tightly against the tooth.

- Gently rub the side of the tooth, moving the floss away from the gum with up-and-down motions.

- Repeat this method on the rest of your teeth. Don't __7__ the back side of your last tooth.

1 a) bathing   b) eating
   c) shouting   d) breathing
        e) swimming

2 a) cities   b) stones
   c) spaces   d) balls
        e) devices

3 a) half   b) above
   c) behind   d) below
        e) all

4 a) washed   b) wet
   c) perfect   d) slimy
        e) dirty

5 a) party   b) skate
   c) remain   d) ride
        e) read

6 a) mother   b) friend
   c) secretary   d) pet
        e) dentist

7 a) embarrass   b) hit
   c) call   d) forget
        e) break

DOGS

Puppies are born ___1___ and deaf. They start to see at about two weeks. They start to hear at about three weeks of age. Puppyhood is a time of rapid growth and development. Puppies require nearly double the amount of nutrients as ___2___ dogs.

Do not let puppies learn any ___3___ behaviors. Do not let them do anything that you would not want them to do as adults. It is much easier to prevent a behavior than to stop it after it ___4___.

The number one mistake people make when trying to train a dog is going too fast. Take it slow. Don't get frustrated. That will just delay the training.

Obesity is the number one nutritional problem in dogs. One in every three dogs is overweight. Purina, a pet food company, conducted a study. The study showed that dogs that ate 25 percent less food than other dogs lived an average of two years longer.

Any dog, even your own, can ___5___ when it is in pain. Therefore you should approach an injured dog very slowly. Be aware that its behavior could be unpredictable.

Panting is considered normal for a dog. Dogs have poorly developed sweat glands. Panting is a way that dogs ___6___ down when they are too hot.

One reason dogs jump on you is to test their position. Letting dogs jump up makes them think they are more powerful than you. Jumping up on people is a hard ___7___ to break. Dogs that jump are at risk of hurting either someone else or themselves.

1 a) old   b) mature
     c) blind   d) lazy
          e) dull

2 a) older   b) younger
     c) smarter   d) smaller
          e) slower

3 a) cute   b) bad
     c) good   d) nice
          e) sweet

4 a) starts   b) returns
     c) turns   d) ends
          e) dissolves

5 a) dance   b) sing
     c) bark   d) bite
          e) sulk

6 a) climb   b) bend
     c) tear   d) get
          e) cool

7 a) box   b) target
     c) bar   d) habit
          e) treat

THE AMERICAN TURTLE

The connection between Connecticut and submarines goes back over 200 years. Connecticut serves as the home for many of the United States Navy's submarines. It is also where many submarines are built.

The first submarine ever to be used in combat was from Connecticut. It was called the American Turtle. David Bushnell designed it to _____1_____ a bomb. The bomb was to be used against an enemy ship during the American Revolution.

1 a) build   b) protest
    c) stop   d) transport
       e) display

The Turtle was tested in the Connecticut River. The tests took place off Old Saybrook. Ezra Bushnell, David's brother, piloted the submarine for the test.

After the tests were _____2_____, the submarine was ready to go into ____3____ on its first combat mission. However, Ezra Bushnell became ill and was unable to participate.

2 a) forgotten   b) successful
    c) deserted   d) advertised
       e) played
3 a) air   b) trucks
    c) battle   d) land
       e) storage

Nevertheless, the American Turtle was launched for its first real fight on September 6, 1776. The pilot was Ezra Lee of Old Lyme, Connecticut.

The Turtle was aimed at the British flagship, the HMS Eagle. The 64-gun enemy ship was docked in the New York harbor. It was anchored off the ____4____ now occupied by the Statue of Liberty.

4 a) reputation   b) island
    c) advice   d) myth
       e) gear

The American Turtle made its way underwater to the rear of the HMS Eagle's hull. The target was the ship's rudder, which steers the ship. A screw was to be used to attach the bomb to the enemy's hull. The pilot needed to find a wooden part of the hull in order to use the screw. Unfortunately, Lee struck metal first. A second attempt also failed.

Lee then led the American Turtle away. It was seen and chased. The bomb was released into the water. It made a huge ____5____. The British knew the American Turtle was trying to attack their ship. They moved the ____6____ away.

5 a) story   b) whale
    c) explosion   d) circle
       d) turn
6 a) fleet   b) city
    c) country   d) town
       e) float

The American Turtle failed to ____7____ its target. However, it had made an impact on the war. General George Washington said, "Bushnell is a man of great mechanical powers. He is fertile in invention and a master of execution."

7 a) win   b) deny
    c) find   d) need
       e) sink

NATURE TOURS

Our tours are limited to 20 people. This is because we like a relaxed, informal atmosphere. We also like a slow pace. The slow pace makes our chance of spotting ____1____ a lot better. The larger the group of people stomping down a forest trail, the less likely it is that wild creatures will be seen. In a small group, each tour member has time to view, photograph, and experience the natural environment fully.

Our tours are designed for active, ____2____ travelers. Participants should be flexible and ready for what you might see in the areas far from the city. Since we travel all over the world, you must be able to adjust to the customs in other ____3____. You must be willing to live within the limits of scheduled group touring.

Our days are ____4____ because we want to show you as much as possible. We often get an early start. While our tours are active, they are not rugged. Field trips usually involve walks of a mile or less. We walk at a slow pace and often stop to take a closer look at the delights nature holds for us.

You are free to skip a walk or an entire field trip. However, if you don't enjoy walking or if you have difficulty walking, our tours are ____5____ for you.

We invite you to explore the world. Nature is full of wonderful ____6____ no matter where you go. In a Costa Rican national park, you might look down to find leafcutter ants parading across your path, or suddenly see a troop of animals moving through the trees.

In Alaska, you might look up to see a bald eagle ____7____ by, or spend half an hour watching a grizzly and her cubs. In Hawaii, you can see Kilauea volcano adding land to our 50th state. You can see how fragile life takes hold on the newest land on earth.

1 a) wildlife   b) land
   c) plants   d) birds
            e) strangers

2 a) scared   b) slow
   c) fearful   d) indifferent
            e) curious

3 a) tours   b) travel
   c) trains   d) barns
            e) countries

4 a) short   b) slow
   c) full   d) few
            e) firm

5 a) best   b) not
   c) right   d) good
            e) great

6 a) machines   b) surprises
   c) places   d) films
            e) liquids

7 a) soaring   b) walking
   c) singing   d) yelling
            e) swimming

33

BARN RAISINGS

Just 100 years ago Enfield, Connecticut had many tobacco farms. Tobacco shed "raisings" were a popular social event looked forward to by young and old alike.

These events let men show off their _____1_____ in competitions against one another. Women had the opportunity to show what good ____2____ they were with pie baking contests. It was an exciting occasion for kids, too.

1 a) baking   b) height
    c) strength   d) money
      e) families

2 a) dancers   b) artists
    c) cooks   d) poets
      e) writers

The ____3____ having the raising did all the work to prepare for building the structure. The ground was leveled and the piers poured. The frame was spiked together in sections. The frame was laid on the ground ready to be raised into position. Rafters and braces were made ready. When everything was arranged, the date was set.

3 a) farmer   b) fighter
    c) soldier   d) fireman
      e) sailor

The neighborhood wives prepared food such as cakes, doughnuts, pies and drinks. On the day of the raising, neighbors and friends from all over met on the site. After much friendly interaction, the men gathered around the frame of the new shed.

They began raising the first section of the frame. At the command of "Heave!" everyone ____4____. The heavy frame section began to rise into place.

4 a) laughed   b) lifted
    c) waved   d) left
      e) fell

After many heaves, the section was finally moved into a standing position and braced in place. Then the whole process was ____5____ with section after section until the whole frame was up, connected, and attached. Next, the rafters and the roof were put on and the raising was over. When each raising was completed, everyone headed for the refreshments.

5 a) taught   b) painted
    c) described   d) graded
      e) repeated

The food was quickly ____6____ up by the large group. While everyone was eating, many exciting moments of the event were relived. The status of the crops, the weather, or the chances of the next political candidate were also ____7____. Finally, one by one, the neighbors left for their own farms.

6 a) pushed   b) spread
    c) thrown   d) gobbled
      e) fixed

7 a) discussed   b) chanted
    c) arranged   d) constructed
      e) broken

34

LOVE CANAL

In the late 1800s, a man called William T. Love decided to build a canal. A canal is a man-made waterway. He wanted to __1__ the upper and lower parts of the Niagara River, separated by Niagra Falls. He began to dig a large pit for his canal. However, Love ran out of money and had to abandon his project before it was finished.

The large pit eventually filled with water and the people of Niagra used it as a giant swimming hole. They named this swimming hole "Love Canal." It soon became a very __2__ spot where many people swam.

In the early 1900s, a company called Hooker Chemical opened a factory right next to Love Canal. They began __3__ chemical waste into the canal. Within months, Love Canal started to smell so bad that people stopped swimming there. The people of Niagara were quite sad. They did not like to see a great swimming hole turn into a big stinky mess.

No one swam in Love Canal anymore. In 1953, the town decided to __4__ the hole with dirt. Then they built a school right on top of what used to be Love Canal.

In the 1970s, a series of powerful rainstorms hit the area. It rained and rained and rained. All of that rain caused much of the waste that had been buried at Love Canal to rise up through the ground.

Things got even worse when the rain carried the waste into nearby creeks and __5__. These events __6__ the people who lived near Love Canal. They asked local officials to come to Niagara. They wanted to make sure that the waste was not putting anyone in danger. Officials searched the area around Love Canal. They realized that the waste there was very dangerous.

At that time, Jimmy Carter was President of the United States. He found out about the mess at Love Canal and asked the government to help people leave the __7__ areas. He told the government to help them find new homes.

1 a) purchase b) bury
c) employ d) connect
e) trade

2 a) scary b) popular
c) cold d) strange
e) shallow

3 a) braking b) chopping
c) selling d) dumping
e) inviting

4 a) fill b) color
c) empty d) clean
e) protect

5 a) prisons b) restaurants
c) packages d) hospitals
e) streams
6 a) excited b) frightened
c) comforted d) helped
e) moved

7 a) empty b) open
c) polluted d) crowded
e) underwater

SEA TURTLES

Long Island Sound is home to a rich marine life. Many of us never see most of this life. Even those of us who live close to the ___1___ may have never seen a seal. Few of us have seen a sea turtle. During the late summer, a wonderful undersea ___2___ happens. Sea turtles travel through the waters off the coast of New England between August and September.

Several kinds of sea turtles swim right by us. The green sea turtle can weigh as much as 500 pounds. They vary in ___3___ from light tan to black. They have a yellow-white underside of their smooth shell.

Kemp's Ridley sea turtle can weigh up to 100 pounds. It is light olive green in color. It is quite rare and one of the most ___4___ sea turtles.

Leatherback sea turtles can weigh up to 1,300 pounds. They have a ridged shell that has a rubber-like texture and is black with white spots. The loggerhead sea turtle weighs up to 450 pounds. It has a square-shaped head and is reddish brown in color.

We have to be careful not to ___5___ these turtles. Power-boaters should take particular care. These air-breathing animals often come to the surface. They can be injured and even killed by propellers from boats.

Sea turtles can also get tangled in fishing ___6___ and lobster pot lines. One of the biggest causes of sea turtle deaths is the accidental swallowing of floating plastic bags. Turtles mistake these bags for jellyfish. Jellyfish are their favorite ___7___. So please use care with your pleasure boats and dispose of your trash properly.

Living by or visiting the coast of Connecticut is a wonderful experience. It is a beautiful habitat full of amazing wildlife. Treat it wisely so we can enjoy it for generations to come!

1 a) mountains   b) desert
   c) prairie   d) city
      e) shore

2 a) show   b) movement
   c) creation   d) disaster
      e) explosion

3 a) age   b) size
   c) height   d) color
      e) length

4 a) endangered   b) happy
   c) plentiful   d) heavy
      e) angry

5 a) hurt   b) avoid
   c) watch   d) help
      e) see

6 a) boats   b) nets
   c) decks   d) bait
      e) pants

7 a) relatives   b) partners
   c) candy   d) food
      e) medicine

BOG CREEK

Bog Creek Farm looked like an average, everyday chicken ranch. However, some people used the farm as a place to dispose of trash. They dumped their old chemicals and paints there. These chemicals were dumped into a 150-foot long trench that ____1____ across the property.

The secret dumping went on for a few years until a neighbor complained to local officials. He did not like the gross ____2____ that kept coming from the property. The officials decided to visit the owner of Bog Creek Farm. They wanted to ____3____ it out for themselves. The owner told the officials that people had always dumped chemicals on his farm.

The officials ____4____ to the owner's story and asked the owner to bulldoze the trench. They ordered him to ship the dirt to a special storage area. The owner agreed. The bad odors continued. The owner left the property and did not come back.

Officials continued to investigate. They began to find more and more chemicals in the farm's soil. They found dead fish in a nearby ____5____. They were alarmed. The officials asked the Environmental Protection Agency, an organization that monitors problems with the environment, to help. They wanted to use the Superfund program.

The Superfund program helps states clean up abandoned polluted areas. Superfund officials began an inspection of Bog Creek Farm. They determined that the farm was very polluted. They found lots of chemicals. It was in need of serious cleanup.

First, Superfund cleanup crews dug up all the polluted soil on the site. Then the Environmental Protection Agency built a special kind of ____6____ called an incinerator. The incinerator at Bog Creek Farm burnt up enough soil to fill 500 tractor-trailers!

Next, Superfund cleanup crews tackled the problem of cleaning up the brooks and rivers near Bog Creek. After a great amount of hard ____7____, they were able to clean everything up.

1 a) landed   b) recorded
  c) stretched   d) fired
        e) flipped

2 a) smells   b) people
  c) plants   d) pigs
        e) water

3 a) cut   b) check
  c) break   d) blank
        e) pry

4 a) rode   b) exercised
  c) planned   d) climbed
        e) listened

5 a) store   b) stream
  c) ranch   d) road
        e) farm

6 a) freezer   b) match
  c) blanket   d) elevator
        e) machine

7 a) rocks   b) work
  c) hammers   d) tools
        e) concrete

37

MONITORING BIRDS

You can help to keep two unique types of birds safe. They are the Whippoorwill and the Common Nighthawk. How can you help? Connecticut officials need ___1___ to participate in a survey about these two birds. All you need is a pencil, a survey sheet, and the willingness to help.

The Whippoorwill's breeding cycle is closely tied in with the cycles of the moon. The eggs usually hatch around the time of a full moon. On most nights, the birds feed on small flying insects. The insects are visible at dawn and at dusk. When there is a full moon, the adult birds can be seen flying through the night sky. They are trying to keep up with the food demands of their baby chicks.

Whippoorwills lay their eggs directly on the ___2___ instead of in a tree. The female incubates these eggs for about 20 days. The female makes no nest. Instead, she is the best camouflage for the eggs because she ___3___ into the leaves. This secretive habit makes finding nesting Whippoorwills extremely ___4___. Luckily these birds call during the evening hours. They haunt the woodlands calling out a "whip-poor-will, whip-poor-will, whip-poor-will" on moonlit nights.

The Common Nighthawk is most active at twilight, just like the Whippoorwill. However, the Nighthawk does not like the open wooded habitats preferred by the Whippoorwill. The Common Nighthawk's commonly preferred habitat is in non-forested open areas.

Historically, the Common Nighthawk looked for open bare earth and grasslands for laying eggs. Now these birds have shifted to using level areas in more urban sites. They raise their chicks on ___5___ gravel roofs so that the eggs won't roll away.

Males attract females at dusk. They do so by calling, circling and then swooping down. They end up almost ___6___ into the female's nest site. It is during this swoop that the male's front feathers on his ___7___ create a loud booming sound. This sound helps to locate them.

Monitoring these two bird species is important to Connecticut wildlife officials. City dwellers might not have thought about having wildlife in their neighborhoods. However, they can also participate in the survey.

1 a) species   b) birds
     c) volunteers   d) babies
              e) vacuums

2 a) ground   b) roof
     c) table   d) lake
              e) foot

3 a) sinks   b) blends
     c) dives   d) paddles
              e) floats

4 a) relaxing   b) easy
     c) odd   d) difficult
              e) expensive

5 a) steep   b) angled
     c) flat   d) slippery
              e) jagged

6 a) spitting   b) crashing
     c) flipping   d) trotting
              e) dancing

7 a) wings   b) shoes
     c) arms   d) palms
              e) knuckles

38

HOUSATONIC RIVER TRIPS

Would you like to enjoy an afternoon on the water? You can go by kayak, canoe or raft. You could even paddle a 10-mile section of the beautiful Housatonic River. The river, located in northwestern Connecticut, is a mixture of moving flat water and moderate white water. This river is suitable for novice paddlers.

The famous covered bridge in West Cornwall marks the halfway point down the river. ____1____ is available at several places there between 12–2 p.m. You may also bring your own picnic.

Stop at one of the many scenic spots along the river. You will complete your _____2_____ 10 miles downstream at Housatonic Meadows Picnic Area.

In the summer months, after spring rains and snowmelt swells the banks of the Housatonic River, a more ___3___ ride is available.

The most challenging section of the river starts at Bulls Bridge Gorge in Kent, Connecticut. You will wind your way through the ___4___ rapids. Skilled ___5___ will expertly take you through the rapids. The rapids have names like the "Flume," "S-Turn," and "Pencil Sharpener."

Bulls Bridge Gorge offers some of the most technically ___6___ rapids in the East. Trips down this section of the river are not for the faint-hearted. You must be 16 years of age or older.

Trips are by ___7___ only. The charge of $85 per person includes wetsuit, all equipment, and lunch. Low water may force trips to be cancelled or moved to a different section of the river.

Bring a change of clothes to leave in the car. You should also bring a towel, and old sneakers or water shoes. You may also need sunblock, bug repellent, eyeglass strap, rain gear and a wool sweater. Also, you may want to bring a waterproof camera.

1 a) Lunch   b) Boating
   c) Admission   d) Wood
          e) Volleyball

2 a) journey   b) dinner
   c) biking   d) journal
          e) dining

3 a) delicate   b) exciting
   c) important   d) bland
          e) simple

4 a) steaming   b) slow
   c) warm   d) surging
          e) lazy
5 a) nurses   b) otters
   c) guides   d) soldiers
          e) fisherman
6 a) easy   b) difficult
   c) slow   d) relaxing
          e) wet
7 a) luck   b) foot
   c) helicopter   d) departure
          e) appointment

ROBERTO CLEMENTE

Roberto Clemente was born in Puerto Rico. He was the youngest of four children. As a boy, Roberto excelled in track and field. He competed in the javelin throw. He also ____1____ races over short distances. He won medals in both racing and the javelin.

1 a) reported   b) saw
    c) ran   d) started
        e) judged

However, Clemente's real love was baseball. He played baseball with the Santurce Crabbers. They were in the Puerto Rican Winter League. He then signed with the Brooklyn Dodgers. He was assigned to play for their top minor league team in Montreal.

In 1954, Roberto Clemente was the number one draft pick in major league baseball. That pick was awarded to the Pittsburgh Pirates. Clemente joined the Pittsburgh Pirates in 1955 and stayed there for his entire ____2____. He played for the Pirates for 18 ____3____, from 1955 to 1972. He was an outstanding outfielder and a great hitter.

2 a) day   b) career
    c) family   d) body
        e) house

3 a) years   b) decades
    c) weeks   d) months
        e) days

Clemente played in two World Series and received many awards during his career. He was the National League batting champion four times. He was awarded 12 Gold Glove trophies. He was selected National League "Most Valuable Player" in both the 1966 and 1971 World Series.

At the end of the 1972 season, Roberto Clemente ____4____ a great goal. He got his 3,000th hit. Very few players get 3,000 hits. It was Clemente's last hit.

4 a) stopped   b) achieved
    c) imagined   d) created
        e) ended

Roberto Clemente ____5____ to help people less fortunate than himself. On New Year's Eve 1972, a plane left for Nicaragua. There had been an earthquake there and Roberto flew there taking medical supplies, food, and clothing. The weather was ____6____, and the plane was unsafe. Roberto Clemente was determined to go anyway.

5 a) refused   b) forgot
    c) seemed   d) appeared
        e) wanted

6 a) great   b) pleasant
    c) nice   d) good
        e) poor

Tragically, the plane ____7____ off the coast of Puerto Rico. Everyone aboard died. Roberto's body was never found. He was a great player and a generous man. Roberto Clemente became a hero to many.

7 a) soared   b) crashed
    c) sailed   d) emptied
        e) landed

THE CHESTER-HADLYME FERRY

The oldest ferry service in Connecticut began operating in 1655. It crossed the Connecticut River.

There were no bridges across the river back then. The ferry was the only way to cross the water. It transported __1__ and horses from Rocky Hill to Glastonbury. It is still operating today. It is open May 1st through October 31st. It now carries cars, too.

The second oldest ferry is the Chester-Hadlyme Ferry which began service in 1769.

Jonathan Warner owned land on both sides of the Connecticut River and operated a ferry. It was called Warner's Ferry and ____2____ King's Highway in Chester to Norwich Road in Lyme. It later became the Chester-Hadlyme Ferry.

The ferry was used throughout the Revolutionary War to ____3____ men and supplies across the river. There were no bridges back then, so the ferry was very important.

The ferry was pushed across the river using long poles. It was very ____4____ work to push a big load.

The ferry was known as Warner's Ferry until 1878. At that time it became the town ferry. In 1882 it was named the Chester-Hadlyme Ferry. In 1917, the ferry was turned over to the government of Connecticut. The Connecticut Department of Transportation now runs it.

The present ferry is called the Selden III. It was built in 1949. The Selden III is an open boat with its own motor. It is 65 feet long and 30 feet wide. The vessel can hold eight to nine cars and 49 ____5____.

The Selden III provides a direct link between Chester and Hadlyme at Route 148. The ferry makes this a very __6__ and stress-free trip. It operates from April 1st through November 30th. It is also a great way to experience ____7____.

1 a) boats   b) water
   c) art   d) people
        e) trains

2 a) flew   b) wrote
   c) marched   d) slid
        e) connected

3 a) carry   b) bully
   c) taunt   d) attack
        e) support

4 a) little   b) sticky
   c) hard   d) expensive
        e) lucky

5 a) trucks   b) pigeons
   c) buses   d) passengers
        e) baskets

6 a) annoying b) easy
   c) far   d) slow
        e) dangerous

7 a) history   b) danger
   c) reality   d) driving
        e) doubt

BLUE JAY ORCHARDS

Blue Jay Orchards is a 140-acre ___1___ that is located in Bethel, Connecticut. It is one of the last commercial orchards in Fairfield County.

The Weed family ___2___ the farm for many years. When her husband died, Elizabeth Weed kept a few cows and sold butter. She churned butter from the cows' milk herself. She also opened her home to New York City vacationers during the summer months. It became one of the area's first Bed and Breakfast hotels. The farm's history as a modern orchard dates back to 1934 when a man named Mr. Josephy bought the farmhouse and 50 acres from Elizabeth Weed.

During the next 50 years, the farm ___3___ from 50 acres to its much larger current size. Josephy acquired the dairy farm across the street. He bought a vegetable farm next to his property. The farmhouses of both farms remain in use today.

Later, Josephy sold the land to the State of Connecticut. It was the first farm to be preserved as farmland in the state. The Patterson family bought Blue Jay Orchards in 1985.

The farm is ___4___ for pick-your-own fun from August through October. The Farm Market Store and Gift Shop operates from August through December. It offers baked goods, apple items, produce, baskets and gifts. The Pattersons also offer the farm for educational school tours. They raise ___5___ for local charities.

Recently, Blue Jay Orchards lost its entire crop. They lost their apple, peach, and pear crops. It was the first time this had happened in 25 years. In early April, ___6___ rose into the mid-90s. That was followed by three nights of temperatures in the mid-20s. This resulted in ___7___ that destroyed all of the young blossoms. This killing frost also destroyed most crops in both Connecticut's and New York's orchards.

1　a) farm　　　　b) factory
　　c) mall　　　　d) restaurant
　　　　e) store

2　a) forgot　　　b) plowed
　　c) rented　　　d) owned
　　　　e) checked

3　a) escaped　　b) moved
　　c) grew　　　　d) stopped
　　　　e) shrunk

4　a) bad　　　　b) open
　　c) closed　　　d) lost
　　　　e) away

5　a) taxes　　　b) alarms
　　c) sails　　　　d) money
　　　　e) flags

6　a) cows　　　　b) temperatures
　　c) plants　　　d) staff
　　　　e) land

7　a) heat　　　　b) warmth
　　c) freezing　　d) flooding
　　　　e) fog

Made in the USA
Las Vegas, NV
19 February 2024

85980644R00031